PREMIER LEAGUE

THE F.A. PREMIER LEAGUE

£4.99

We are now into the third season of the FA Premier League - and it's time to welcome you to the very first Premier League Annual specifically aimed at younger football fans. You are very important to us and we hope you will grow up sharing our love of the game.

The Annual is packed with stunning pictures and information on all the current Premier League clubs, including their addresses and telephone numbers, their honours and the facts and figures of their 1993-94 performance.

There are also features on the background of the FA Premier League, the FA Carling Premiership campaign, the relegation and promotion battles, the leading scorers and all the other players who really stood out last season.

And there's a brilliant competition in which YOU could win amongst other prizes an official Mitre football as played with by your footballing heroes.

Of course, today's children will be tomorrow's supporters - and tomorrow's players.

We are putting a great deal of time and resources into improving the ways in which our clubs work with 9-16 year-olds. We recognise how important it is to ensure that we provide the best possible coaching for talented players and look forward to this investment paying off over the years.

We hope you enjoy this Annual, and we hope you will continue to enjoy all the exciting football played by the top 22 clubs in the country.

Rick Parry

RICK PARRY, Chief Executive, FA Premier League.

CONTENTS

THE F.A. PREMIER LEAGUE

© The F.A. Premier League 1994

* Written and compiled by Tony Lynch * Edited by Melanie J Clayden * Photographs by Action Images * Designed by Louise Ivimy, Susan Bartram and Joanna Davies * Thanks to Rick Parry, Adrian Cook and Richard Carpenter of the FA Premier League
* All facts believed correct at time of going to press *

Published by Grandreams Ltd, Jadwin House, 205-211 Kentish Town Road, London NW5 2JU.

* Printed in Italy *

ARSENAL

Arsenal Stadium, Highbury,
London, N5 1BU.
Telephone: 071-226 0304
Fax: 071-226 0329
Ticket Information: 071-359 0131

Chairman: P D Hill-Wood
Chief Executive/Secretary: K J Friar
Team Manager: George Graham
Sponsors: JVC
Nickname: The Gunners'
Team Colours: Red shirts with
white sleeves, white shorts, red
socks
Change Colours: Yellow and blue
shirts, blue shorts, yellow socks
Pitch dimensions: 110 x 73yds
Ground Capacity: 38,000

HONOURS

League Champions: 1930-31,
1932-33, 1933-34, 1934-35,
1937-38, 1947-48, 1952-53, 1970-
71, 1988-89, 1990-91 (10)
FA Cup Winners: 1930, 1936, 1950,
1971, 1979, 1993 (6)
League Cup Winners: 1987, 1993
(2)
Charity Shield Winners: 1930,
1931, 1933, 1934, 1938, 1948,
1953, 1991 - shared (8)
*European Cup-Winners' Cup
Winners:* 1994 (1)
UEFA Cup Winners: 1970 (1)

PREMIERSHIP PERFORMANCE 1993-94

P	W	D	L	F	A	GD	Pts	Pos
42	18	17	7	53	28	+25	71	4th

Leading Scorer:	Ian Wright (23)
Average Attendance:	30,492
Highest Attendance:	36,203

Squad Stats (*Matches started - Sub played - Sub not played - Goals*):
Tony Adams 35-0-0-1, Steve Bould 23-2-2-1, Kevin Campbell 28-9-2-14, Paul Davis 21-
1-2-0, Paul Dickov 0-1-0-0, Lee Dixon 32-1-0-0, Mark Flatts 2-1-0-0, Neil Heaney 1-0-
0-0, David Hillier 11-4-1-0, John Jensen 27-0-0-0, Martin Keown 23-10-3-0, Anders
Limpar 9-1-2-0, Andy Linighan 20-1-3-0, Pal Lydersen 0-0-1-0, Eddie McGoldrick 23-3-
2-0, Paul Merson 24-9-1-6, Alan Miller 3-1-37-0, Steve Morrow 7-4-2-0, Ray Parlour 24-
3-2-2, David Seaman 39-0-0-0, Ian Selley 16-2-5-0, Alan Smith 21-4-2-3, James Will 0-
0-5-0, Nigel Winterburn 34-0-0-0, Ian Wright 39-0-0-23.

ASTON VILLA

Chairman: H D Ellis
Secretary: S M Stride
Team Manager: Ron Atkinson
Sponsors: Muller
Nickname: 'The Villans'
Team Colours: Claret shirts with sky blue trim, white shorts, white and claret socks
Change Colours: Green, black and red striped shirts, black shorts, black and green socks
Pitch dimensions: 115 x 75yds
Ground Capacity: 40,000

Villa Park, Birmingham, B6.
Telephone: 021-327 2299
Fax: 021-322 2107
Ticket Information: 021-327 5353
Souvenir Shop: 021-327 2800

PREMIERSHIP PERFORMANCE 1993-94

P	W	D	L	F	A	GD	Pts	Pos
42	15	12	15	46	50	-4	57	10th

Leading Scorer: Dean Saunders (10)
Average Attendance: 28,697
Highest Attendance: 45,347

Squad Stats (*Matches started - Sub played - Sub not played - Goals*):
Dalian Atkinson 29-0-0-8, Earl Barrett 39-0-0-0, Stefan Beinlich 6-1-2-1, Mark Bosnich 28-0-8-0, Mattia Breitkreutz 1-1-0-0, Gordon Cowans 9-2-1-0, Neil Cox 16-4-11-2, Tony Daley 19-8-0-1, Ugo Ehiogu 14-3-6-0, David Farrell 4-0-1-0, Graham Fenton 9-3-0-1, Steve Froggatt 8-1-0-1, Ray Houghton 25-5-0-2, Dariusz Kubicki 1-1-0-0, Paul McGrath 30-0-0-1, Mike Oakes 0-0-8-0, Garry Parker 17-2-1-2, Kevin Richardson 40-0-0-5, Dean Saunders 37-1-1-10, Bryan Small 8-1-2-0, Nigel Spink 14-1-24-0, Steve Staunton 24-0-0-2, Shaun Teale 37-1-0-1, Andy Townsend 32-0-0-3, Guy Whittingham 13-5-6-3, Dwight Yorke 2-10-3-2.

HONOURS

League Champions: 1893-94, 1895-96, 1896-97, 1898-99, 1899-1900, 1909-10, 1980-81 (7)
FA Cup Winners: 1887, 1895, 1897, 1905, 1913, 1920, 1957 (7)
League Cup Winners: 1961, 1975, 1977, 1994 (4)
Charity Shield Winners: 1981 - shared (1)
European Cup Winners: 1982 (1)
European Super Cup Winners: 1982 (1)

BLACKBURN ROVERS

ARTE ET LABORE

Ewood Park, Blackburn, BB2 4JF.
Telephone: 0254 698888
Fax: 0254 671042
Club Shop: 0254 672137

Chairman: R D Coar BSc
Secretary: J W Howarth
Team Manager: Kenny Dalglish
Sponsors: McEwans
Nickname: 'Rovers'
Team Colours: Royal blue and white halved shirts, white shorts, blue socks with white trim
Change Colours: Red and black striped shirts, black shorts, black socks
Pitch dimensions: 115 x 72yds
Ground Capacity: 18,000

PREMIERSHIP PERFORMANCE 1993-94

P	W	D	L	F	A	GD	Pts	Pos
42	25	9	8	63	36	+27	84	2nd

Leading Scorer:	Alan Shearer (31)
Average Attendance:	17,303
Highest Attendance:	21,462

Squad Stats (*Matches started - Sub played - Sub not played - Goals*):
Patrik Andersson 1-0-2-0, Mark Atkins 8-7-5-1, David Batty 26-0-0-0, Henning Berg 38-3-0-1, Tim Flowers 29-0-0-0, Kevin Gallacher 27-3-0-7, Colin Hendry 22-1-0-0, Graeme Le Saux 40-1-0-2, Lee Makel 0-2-0-0, Nick Marker 16-7-9-0, David May 40-0-0-1, Bobby Mimms 13-0-29-0, Kevin Moran 19-0-0-1, Andy Morrison 1-4-1-0, Mike Newell 27-1-0-6, Ian Pearce 1-4-5-1, Stuart Ripley 40-0-0-4, Alan Shearer 34-6-1-31, Tim Sherwood 38-0-0-2, Francesco Talia 0-0-13-0, Paul Warhurst 4-5-2-0, Jason Wilcox 31-2-1-6, Alan Wright 7-5-7-0.

HONOURS

League Champions: 1911-12, 1913-14 (2)
FA Cup Winners: 1884, 1885, 1886, 1890, 1891, 1928 (6)
Charity Shield Winners: 1912 (1)

CHELSEA

Stamford Bridge, Fulham Road,
London, SW6 1HS.
Telephone: 071-385 5545
Fax: 071-381 4831
Ticket Information: 0891 121011
Club Shop: 071-381 4569

HONOURS
League Champions: 1954-55 (1)
FA Cup Winners: 1970 (1)
League Cup Winners: 1965 (1)
Charity Shield Winners: 1955 (1)
*European Cup-Winners' Cup
winners:* 1971 (1)

PREMIERSHIP PERFORMANCE 1993-94

P	W	D	L	F	A	GD	Pts	Pos
42	13	12	17	49	53	-4	51	14th

Leading Scorer: Mark Stein (13)
Average Attendance: 19,211
Highest Attendance: 37,064

Squad Stats (*Matches started - Sub played - Sub not played - Goals*):
Darren Barnard 9-3-3-1, Craig Burley 20-3-0-3, Tony Cascarino 16-4-2-4, Steve Clarke 39-0-0-0, Nick Colgan 0-0-2-0, Mal Donaghy 24-4-1-1, Andy Dow 13-1-0-0, Mike Duberry 1-0-2-0, Robert Fleck 7-2-0-1, Gareth Hall 4-3-2-0, Kevin Hitchcock 2-0-40-0, Glenn Hoddle 16-3-2-1, David Hopkin 12-9-0-1, Erland Johnsen 27-1-1-1, Dimitri Kharine 40-0-0-0, Jakob Kjeldbjerg 29-0-1-1, David Lee 3-4-2-1, Andy Myers 6-0-0-0, Eddie Newton 33-3-0-0, Gavin Peacock 37-0-0-8, Neil Shipperley 18-6-1-4, Frank Sinclair 35-0-0-0, Nigel Spackman 5-2-9-0, John Spencer 13-5-5-5, Mark Stein 18-0-0-13, Dennis Wise 35-0-0-4.

Chairman: K W Bates
Secretary: C Hutchinson
Match Secretary: K Lacy
Team Manager: Glenn Hoddle
Sponsors: Coors
Nickname: 'The Blues'
Team Colours: All blue shirts and shorts with red trim, white socks with red and blue trim
Change Colours: White shirts with red pinstripe and blue trim, red shorts, red socks
Pitch dimensions: 110 x 73yds
Ground Capacity: 37,605

THE STORY OF THE PREMIER LEAGUE

THE F.A. PREMIER LEAGUE

For many, many years there had been much talk among football folk about the streamlining of the top division of the Football League.

Our clubs and players had long been complaining that they were playing too many matches in a season, especially in comparison with most other European nations. What's more, this 'over-playing' was having a negative effect on the performance of the national team.

It was felt that the eventual reduction to eighteen clubs could only be good for the English game.

After a great deal of speculation, things really began to move in April 1991 when the FA held a secret meeting, with all the then-First Division clubs, at which they outlined the concept of the proposed new 18-club League.

In May the FA met with ALL the clubs to ask their approval of the idea. This was given, although a compromise was reached on the number of clubs competing - twenty-two was the starting figure eventually agreed upon.

Throughout the summer of 1991 several more meetings were held, about the formation of the new

League's rules and regulations, its voting system and the distribution of future television revenue.

Then, in July, The Football League began a High Court action in an attempt to halt the formation of the Premier League. The legal wrangles went on for a month with the judge eventually deciding that the FA could proceed with its plans. By September the Football League had agreed to the Premier League starting within a year.

However, a lot more behind the scenes work was still to be done and it wasn't until February 1992 that the FA Council finally gave its backing to the new League which would be run as a limited company outside of the FA.

A month later, the highly respected Professional Footballers' Association had their say in the matter, but strike action by the players was eventually averted when the PFA was guaranteed a bigger share of the television revenue.

In May 1992, the Premier League struck a £304 million television deal - the biggest of its kind - with BSkyB and the BBC. In return Sky would screen up to 60 live matches per season and we would see the return of the BBC's popular *Match of the Day* on Saturdays.

And so, at 3.00pm on 15 August 1992, the first nine fixtures of the brand new

Brian Deane, then of Sheffield United, scored the Premier League's first-ever goal in August 1992

Premier League kicked-off. A little over five minutes later, Brian Deane, playing for Sheffield United against Manchester United at Bramall Lane, scored the first Premier League goal - a header - in a 2-1 victory.

Almost ten months later, that defeat was a distant memory as Alex Ferguson's Manchester United were crowned as the Premier League's first ever Champions.

For the second season, 1993-94, Carling teamed up with the Premier League in a £12 million sponsorship deal and the tournament became known as the Carling Premiership. And, as we all know, Manchester United once again topped the table.

At the end of the 1994-95 season, four clubs will be relegated and only two promoted from the First Division, thereby reducing the Premiership to twenty clubs. So, the relegation battles will be even more exciting as the danger-zone clubs battle for those precious points.

COVENTRY CITY

Chairman: B A Richardson
Secretary: G P Hover
Team Manager: Phil Neal
Sponsors: Peugeot
Nickname: 'Sky Blues'
Team Colours: All sky blue, with navy trim
Change Colours: Yellow shirts and navy trim, navy shorts, yellow and navy socks
Pitch dimensions: 110 x 75yds
Ground Capacity: 23,200

HONOURS

FA Cup Winners: 1987 (1)

PREMIERSHIP PERFORMANCE 1993-94

P	W	D	L	F	A	GD	Pts	Pos
42	14	14	14	43	45	-2	56	11th

Leading Scorer: Peter Ndlovu (11)
Average Attendance: 13,564
Highest Attendance: 17,020

Squad Stats (*Matches started - Sub played - Sub not played - Goals*):
Pete Atherton 39-1-1-0, Phil Babb 40-0-0-3, Willie Boland 24-3-3-0, Martyn Booty 2-0-0-0, Brian Borrows 29-0-0-0, David Busst 2-1-2-0, Richard Dalton 0-0-1-0, Julian Darby 25-1-2-5, Martin Davies 0-0-1-0, Sean Flynn 33-3-0-3, John Gayle 3-0-2-0, Jon Gould 9-0-32-0, Mick Harford 0-1-1-1, Leigh Jenkinson 10-6-2-0, Zbignie Kruszynski 1-1-0-0, Chris Marsden 5-2-2-0, Lloyd McGrath 10-1-1-0, Steve Morgan 39-1-0-2, Peter Ndlovu 40-0-0-11, Steve Ogrisovic 33-0-8-0, Ally Pickering 1-3-5-0, Mick Quinn 28-4-7-8, David Rennie 34-0-2-1, Alex Robertson 0-3-4-0, Stewart Robson 1-0-0-0, Tony Sheridan 4-4-1-0, Roy Wegerle 20-1-0-6, John Williams 27-5-1-3, Paul Williams 3-6-1-0.

Highfield Road Stadium, King Richard Street, Coventry, CV2 4FW.
Telephone: 0203 223535
Fax: 0203 630318
Ticket Information: 0203 225545
Souvenir Shop: 0203 257707

CRYSTAL PALACE

Chairman: R G Noades
Secretary: M Hurst
Team Manager: Alan Smith
Sponsors: TDK
Nickname: 'The Eagles'
Team Colours: Red and blue shirts, red shorts, red socks
Change Colours: All white with red and blue trim
Pitch dimensions: 110 x 74yds
Ground Capacity: 27,119

Selhurst Park, London, SE25 6PU.
Telephone: 081-653 1000
Fax: 081-653 6321
Ticket Information: 0891 400 334
Club Shop: 081-653 5584

FIRST DIVISION PERFORMANCE 1993-94

P	W	D	L	F	A	GD	Pts	Pos
46	27	9	10	73	46	+27	90	1st

Leading Scorer: Chris Armstrong (23)
Average Attendance: 15,314
Highest Attendance: 28,749

Palace bounced straight back to the Premiership after being relegated in '92-93. And they came back in real style as First Division Champions.

HONOURS

Division One best season 3rd in 1990-91

13

EVERTON

Goodison Park, Liverpool, L4 4EL.
Telephone: 051-521 2020
Fax: 051-523 9666
Ticket Information: 051-523 6666

PREMIERSHIP PERFORMANCE 1993-94

P	W	D	L	F	A	GD	Pts	Pos
42	12	8	22	42	63	-21	44	17th

Leading Scorer: Tony Cottee (16)
Average Attendance: 22,900
Highest Attendance: 38,157

Squad Stats (*Matches started - Sub played - Sub not played - Goals*):
Gary Ablett 32-0-0-1, Brett Angell 13-3-2-1, Stuart Barlow 5-17-3-3, Peter Beagrie 28-0-0-3, Tony Cottee 36-3-1-16, John Ebbrell 39-0-0-4, Tony Grant 0-0-1-0, Andy Hinchcliffe 26-1-0-0, Paul Holmes 14-0-1-0, Barry Horne 29-3-3-1, Matt Jackson 37-1-0-0, Jason Kearton 0-0-41-0, Anders Limpar 9-0-0-0, Neil Moore 4-0-1-0, Joe Parkinson 0-0-1-0, Pred Radosavljevic 9-14-5-1, Steve Reeves 0-0-1-0, Paul Rideout 21-3-0-6, Gary Rowett 0-2-2-0, Ian Snodin 29-1-1-0, Neville Southall 42-0-0-0, Graham Stuart 26-4-1-3, David Unsworth 7-1-2-0, Mark Ward 26-1-0-1, Robert Warzycha 3-4-1-0, Dave Watson 27-1-0-1.

Chairman: Kenwright/Johnson
Chief Executive/Secretary:
J Greenwood
Team Manager: Mike Walker
Sponsors: NEC
Nickname: 'The Toffees'
Team Colours: Royal blue shirts, white shorts, white socks
Change Colours: Salmon and dark blue striped shirts, dark blue shorts, salmon socks
Pitch dimensions: 112 x 78yds
Ground Capacity: 40,100

HONOURS

League Champions: 1890-91, 1914-15, 1927-28, 1931-32, 1938-39, 1962-63, 1969-70, 1984-85, 1986-87 (9)
FA Cup Winners: 1906, 1933, 1966, 1984 (4)
Charity Shield Winners: 1928, 1932, 1963, 1970, 1984, 1985, 1986 - shared, 1987 (8)
European Cup-Winners' Cup Winners: 1985 (1)

IPSWICH TOWN

Portman Road, Ipswich, IP1 2DA.
Telephone: 0473 219211
Fax: 0473 226835
Ticket Information: 0473 221133
Club Shop: 0473 214641

Chairman: J Kerr MBE JP
Secretary: DC Rose
Team Manager: John Lyall
Sponsors: Fisons
Nickname: 'Town'
Team Colours: Blue shirts with white sleeves, white shorts, blue and white socks
Change Colours: Red shirts and black trim, black shorts, red socks
Pitch dimensions: 112 x 72yds
Ground Capacity: 22,500

PREMIERSHIP PERFORMANCE 1993-94

P	W	D	L	F	A	GD	Pts	Pos
42	9	16	17	35	58	-23	43	19th

Leading Scorer: Ian Marshall (10)
Average Attendance: 16,411
Highest Attendance: 22,559

Squad Stats (*Matches started - Sub played - Sub not played - Goals*):
Clive Baker 15-0-26-0, Lee Durrant 3-4-1-0, Craig Forrest 27-0-3-0, Paul Goddard 3-1-1-0, Dave Gregory 0-0-2-0, Bontcho Guentchev 9-15-6-2, Gavin Johnson 16-0-0-1, Chris Kiwomya 34-3-0-5, David Linighan 38-0-2-3, Ian Marshall 28-1-0-10, Paul Mason 18-4-2-3, Simon Milton 11-4-1-1, Phil Morgan 0-0-13-0, Steve Palmer 31-5-1-1, Stuart Slater 28-0-0-1, Mick Stockwell 42-0-0-3, Neil Thompson 32-0-1-0, John Wark 38-0-0-3, Phil Whelan 28-1-0-0, Steve Whitton 7-4-8-1, David Williams 34-0-0-0, Frank Yallop 2-5-6-0, Eddie Youds 18-5-1-1

HONOURS
League Champions: 1961-62 (1)
FA Cup Winers: 1978 (1)
UEFA Cup Winners: 1981 (1)

15

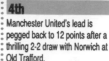

AUG	SEPT	OCT	NOV	DEC

AUG

14th
Kick-off of the second Premier League campaign. The ten matches played produce 27 goals, and were watched by a total of 266,116 fans. Aston Villa enjoyed the biggest victory of the day - 4-1 at home to QPR. Coventry's Mick Quinn hits a hat-trick in a 3-0 home win over Arsenal, and Swindon suffer a 3-1 defeat on their Premiership debut, away to Sheffield Wednesday.

15th
Manchester United begin their defence of the title in a televised encounter against Norwich at Carrow Road. United win 2-0 with goals by Ryan Giggs and Bryan Robson.

18th
Roy Keane, the Premiership's most expensive player, scores twice on his home debut for Manchester United - a 3-0 win against Sheffield United.

21st
Sheffield United are on the wrong end of a 4-2 scoreline against Everton with Tony Cottee scoring a brilliant hat-trick. Norwich's Jeremy Goss scores one of the best goals of the season - a blistering volley in a 4-0 away defeat of Leeds.

25th
Spurs beat Liverpool at Anfield for only the third time in 81 years. West Ham notch their first win of the season, 2-0 at home to Sheffield Wednesday, both goals are scored by Clive Allen. Swindon lose 5-1 away to Southampton.

28th
Ian Rush scores his 200th League goal for Liverpool, in a 2-0 defeat of Leeds. As the month draws to a close Manchester United are sitting on top of the table, just ahead of Liverpool and Arsenal. Swindon are firmly rooted at the bottom with only a single point from five games.

SEPT

11th
Manchester United suffer their first defeat for six months, losing to Chelsea at Stamford Bridge as Gavin Peacock scores the only goal of the game. Kevin Campbell hits a hat-trick for Arsenal in a 4-0 demolition of Ipswich at Highbury. Sheffield United have two players sent off, but still manage a 2-2 draw at home to Spurs.

18th
Coventry remain the only unbeaten side in the Premiership after a 1-1 draw with Chelsea. Blackburn miss out on a top spot after a 2-0 defeat by West Ham.

19th
Manchester United consolidate their position at the top with a 1-0 away victory over Arsenal, thanks to a superstrike by Eric Cantona.

25th
A 2-0 home win over West Ham extends Newcastle's unbeaten run to eight games. Andy Cole takes his goal tally into double figures, while Hammers new Dutch signing Jerone Boere is sent-off only minutes into his debut for the club. Norwich thrash Everton 5-1 at Goodison Park - Efan Ekoku scores four.

OCT

2nd
Gary Speed and Gary McAllister score two goals apiece as Leeds beat Wimbledon 4-0 at Elland Road. Peter Reid makes his debut for Southampton after leaving his player-manager post at Manchester City.

16th
A 2-1 victory by QPR brings Newcastle's 11-match unbeaten run to an end, at St James' Park.

23rd
Alan Shearer scores all three of Blackburn's goals in a 3-3 away draw with Leeds. QPR thrash Coventry 5-1 at Loftus Road.

24th
Matthew Le Tissier makes a comeback for Southampton and scores two cracking goals in a 2-1 home win over Newcastle.

30th
Robbie Fowler hits a hat-trick for Liverpool in a 4-2 victory over Southampton at Anfield. Peter Beardsley also scores three in Newcastle's 4-0 home drubbing of Wimbledon. After a home win over QPR, Manchester United take their tally to 34 points. United are now 11 points clear of closest rivals Norwich, Arsenal, Blackburn and Villa.

NOV

20th
Alan Shearer scores both goals in Blackburn's 2-0 defeat of his old club Southampton at Ewood Park, while former Saints keeper Tim Flowers makes his debut for Rovers.

21st
Andy Cole hits a hat-trick in Newcastle's 3-0 home victory over Liverpool.

24th
Swindon achieve their first-ever Premiership victory, 1-0 at home to QPR. Keith Scott scores the goal.

27th
Manchester United go further ahead at the top of the table, extending their lead to 14 points after a 1-0 away defeat of Coventry.

DEC

4th
Manchester United's lead is pegged back to 12 points after a thrilling 2-2 draw with Norwich at Old Trafford.

8th
QPR have two players sent off in a 3-2 defeat by Liverpool at Anfield. Sheffield Wednesday extend their unbeaten run to 13 games with a 2-2 draw away to Aston Villa.

11th
Andy Cole notches his 23rd goal of the season in Newcastle's 1-1 away draw with Manchester United. Alan Shearer scores his 16th in Blackburn's 2-1 away win over Oldham. Swindon almost beat Liverpool at Anfield, but a late header from Mark Wright levels the scores at 2-2.

18th
Peter Beardsley scores in Newcastle's 2-0 defeat of his old club Everton at Goodison Park. Swindon collect three points for only the second time in the Premiership, with a 2-1 home win against Southampton.

19th
Manchester United score two goals in injury time to beat Aston Villa 3-1 at Old Trafford. United are now 13 points ahead in the title race.

26th
An exciting Boxing Day game at Old Trafford sees Manchester United and Blackburn emerge all-square at 1-1, although Rovers led for 88 minutes of the match.

27th
Kevin Campbell nets his second hat-trick of the season, in Arsenal's 4-0 drubbing of Swindon at the County Ground. Ex-Stoke City striker Mark Stein scores his first goal for Chelsea in a 3-1 defeat by Southampton at The Dell.

29th
A 7-goal thriller at Oldham's Boundary Park, sees Manchester United come out on top, at 5-2. Kevin Campbell is again on target for Arsenal, scoring twice in a 3-0 home win over Sheffield United. Alan Shearer also gets a brace in Blackburn's 2-0 home win against Everton.

JAN | FEB | MAR | APR | MAY

JAN

1st

After the first Premiership games of 1994, Manchester United lead the table with 57 points. Blackburn are second on 45 points. Swindon remain rooted to the bottom with just 15 points.

4th

Liverpool and Manchester United act out a 6-goal drama at Anfield. United are three-up within the first 23 minutes, but the home side battle back to level the scores, in what is dubbed 'the game of the season'.

15th

Everton defeat Swindon 6-2 at Goodison Park, a scoreline which includes a Tony Cottee hat-trick. Swindon's Andy Mutch is sent-off.

22nd

A one minute silent tribute to the late Sir Matt Busby is given by the 44,750 crowd at Old Trafford, before Manchester United's 1-0 victory over Everton. Swindon chalk up their third win of the season - 2-1 at home to Spurs.

FEB

5th

Chelsea's Mark Stein scores twice in a 4-2 defeat by Everton at Goodison Park. It is his tenth goal in seven successive League games, a Premiership record. Manchester United's 3-2 victory away to QPR is their 30th game unbeaten. Jan Fjortoft hits a hat-trick for Swindon in a 3-2 home win against Coventry.

12th

Wimbledon beat Newcastle 4-2 at Selhurst Park. Spurs suffer their sixth successive defeat, at the hands of Blackburn who win 2-0 at White Hart Lane.

14th

A Matthew Le Tissier hat-trick helps Southampton to chalk-up a 4-2 St Valentine's Day massacre of Liverpool at The Dell.

26th

West Ham old-boy Paul Ince saves the day for Manchester United with a late goal in a 2-2 draw at Upton Park. United are now just seven points ahead of Blackburn.

27th

Chelsea beat Spurs 4-3 in a thrilling London derby at Stamford Bridge.

MAR

5th

Chelsea chalk-up their second Premiership victory over leaders Manchester United at Old Trafford. Once again Gavin Peacock hits the winner. Blackburn beat Liverpool 2-0 at Ewood Park to keep up their title challenge. Ian Wright hits a hat-trick as Arsenal thrash Ipswich 5-1 at Portman Road.

12th

Newcastle inflict a 7-1 defeat on Swindon at St James' Park. QPR win a thriller away to Norwich, by the odd goal in seven.

16th

Manchester United thrash Sheffield Wednesday 5-0 at Old Trafford.

22nd

Eric Cantona is sent off in Manchester United's 2-2 draw with Arsenal at Highbury.

26th

Glenn Hoddle scores his first goal for Chelsea, in a 2-0 home defeat of West Ham. Blackburn move to within three points of Manchester United, thanks to a 3-1 win over Swindon.

29th

Sheffield Wednesday collect three points for the first time in nine matches - a 3-1 home win over Chelsea. Manchester United return to the challenge with a 1-0 home defeat of Liverpool.

APR

2nd

At the top of the table Blackburn beat Manchester United 2-0. Manchester City chalk-up their best win of the season, 3-0 at home to Aston Villa. Oldham beat QPR 4-1 at Boundary Park. West Ham's 2-1 home win against Ipswich is their first Premiership victory of the year.

4th

Everton suffer their fifth defeat in six games - a 3-0 home drubbing by high-flying Blackburn. Leeds beat QPR 4-0 at Loftus Road. Manchester City score their first away win in seven months with a 1-0 defeat of Southampton. West Ham crush struggling Spurs 4-1 at White Hart Lane.

9th

Southampton enjoy the best of a 9-goal thriller away to Norwich. Matthew Le Tissier hits a hat-trick in the 5-4 victory. Spurs plunge deeper into trouble with a 1-0 away defeat by Coventry.

11th

Blackburn pull level with Manchester United thanks to a 1-0 home win over Aston Villa.

16th

Andy Cole equals Newcastle's club record of 39 goals in a season with his strike in the 2-0 away win over Liverpool. Wimbledon beat Manchester United 1-0 at Selhurst Park.

23rd

Eric Cantona returns to the Manchester United line up and scores both United's goals in a local derby victory over Manchester City. Swindon are doomed to relegation after a 4-2 home defeat by Wimbledon. Sheffield Wednesday thrash Ipswich 5-0. Spurs grab three valuable points with a 3-0 home win over Southampton.

26th

Wimbledon add to Oldham's relegation worries with a 3-0 win at Selhurst Park.

27th

Manchester United are back in top gear with a 2-0 away win against Leeds. But Blackburn keep up the pressure with a 2-1 win over West Ham. Newcastle beat Aston Villa 5-1 at St James' Park.

30th

Everton are in danger of relegation following a 3-0 away defeat by Leeds. Sheffield United lift themselves out of the bottom three with a 2-0 home victory against Newcastle. Southampton beat Villa 4-1 at the Dell.

MAY

1st

Manchester United tighten the screw at the top of the table with a 2-1 away win over Ipswich.

2nd

The Premiership title race is decided when Coventry beat Blackburn 2-1 at Highfield Road. Rovers can no longer catch Manchester United.

3rd

Fellow strugglers Oldham and Sheffield United share the points in a 1-1 draw at Bramall Lane.

5th

Spurs secure their Premiership future with a 2-0 away win against doom-laden Oldham.

7th

Second-placed Blackburn end their season with a 0-0 draw at home to Ipswich, the point is enough to save the East Anglian club from relegation. Everton save themselves with a 3-2 home win over Wimbledon - but they leave it very, very late. Southampton stay up, thanks to a Matthew Le Tissier-inspired 3-3 draw against West Ham at Upton Park. Oldham go down fighting in a 1-1 away draw with Norwich. Sheffield United lose their Premiership place when Mark Stein hits a last-minute winner for Chelsea in a 3-2 win.

8th

In what proves to be Bryan Robson's last game for the club, an ecstatic Manchester United receive the Premiership trophy after a 0-0 draw with Coventry at Old Trafford. The single point takes United's tally to a Premiership record of 92.

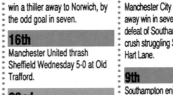

17

F.A. CARLING PREMIERSHIP FACTS & FIGURES 1993-94

BIGGEST WINS

Home

Newcastle	7	Swindon Town	1
Everton	6	Swindon Town	2
Aston Villa	5	Swindon Town	0
Manchester United	5	Sheffield Wednesday	0
Sheffield Wednesday	5	Ipswich Town	0
Sheffield Wednesday	5	West Ham United	0
Tottenham Hotspur	5	Oldham Athletic	0

Away

Swindon Town	0	Liverpool	5
Swindon Town	1	Leeds United	5
Ipswich	1	Arsenal	5
Everton	1	Norwich City	5
Oldham Athletic	2	Manchester United	5

WORST DISCIPLINARY RECORDS

	Booked	Sent Off
Sheffield Utd	45	4
Southampton	45	1
Swindon Town	41	2
Oldham Athletic	31	4

BEST DISCIPLINARY RECORDS

	Booked	Sent Off
Coventry City	15	0
Aston Villa	23	1
Newcastle United	23	1
Sheffield Wed	21	2
Ipswich Town	26	0

ATTENDANCES

TOTAL ATTENDANCE	10,640,528
HIGHEST	45,347 Aston Villa v Liverpool
LOWEST	4,739 Wimbledon v Coventry City

HIGHEST AVERAGE ATTENDANCES

44,244 Manchester United

38,503 Liverpool

36,368 Leeds United

33,792 Newcastle United

30,492 Arsenal

MOST GOALS IN A GAME

9	Norwich City	4	Southampton	5
8	Everton	6	Swindon Town	2
	Newcastle United	7	Swindon Town	1
7	Chelsea	4	Tottenham Hotspur	3
	Norwich City	3	Queens Park Rangers	4
	Oldham Athletic	2	Manchester United	5

MOST GOALS SCORED

Newcastle United	82
Manchester United	80
Sheffield Wednesday	76
Leeds United	65
Norwich City	65

LEAST GOALS SCORED

Ipswich	35
Manchester City	38
Sheffield United	42
Oldham Athletic	42
Everton	42

FINAL TABLE

CLUB	PLAYED	WON	DRAWN	LOST	FOR	AGAINST	GOAL DIFFERENCE	POINTS	COMMENTS
MANCHESTER UNITED	42	27	11	4	80	38	+42	92	A magnificent season for Alex Ferguson's all-star team. They led the Premiership almost from the word go and then rounded-off the most successful season in their history with an FA Cup Final victory. Only the sixth club in history to complete the 'double'.
BLACKBURN ROVERS	42	25	9	8	63	36	+27	84	Kenny Dalglish's Rovers gave United a real run for their money in the closing months of the season and are well worthy of their UEFA Cup berth.
NEWCASTLE UNITED	42	23	8	11	82	41	+41	77	Goals, goals, goals were the order of the day for Kevin Keegan's Magpies - they scored more of them than any other side in the Premiership and enjoyed a goal difference second only to the Champions. Andy Cole was the Premiership's top scorer with 34 successful strikes.
ARSENAL	42	18	17	7	53	28	+25	71	The Gunners had a great season in which they conceded fewer goals than any other Premiership club. They also enjoyed a long unbeaten run. Arsenal flew the English flag in Europe and came back with some silverware, thanks to a solid victory performance over Parma in the Cup-Winners' Cup Final.
LEEDS UNITED	42	18	16	8	65	39	+26	70	Howard Wilkinson must be absolutely delighted with United's much-improved away record. It contributed to a far better performance than in 1992-93 for the Elland Road club.
WIMBLEDON	42	18	11	13	56	53	+3	65	The gates improved at Selhurst Park with an average of more than 10,000, as Joe Kinnear steered his underrated Dons to a top six spot with some brilliant victories over more fancied clubs. No-one can afford to ignore Wimbledon in future.
SHEFFIELD WEDNESDAY	42	16	16	10	76	54	+22	64	Started the campaign slowly, but a good second half to the season lifted Trevor Francis' Owls to the safety of the Premiership's upper reaches.
LIVERPOOL	42	17	9	16	59	55	+4	60	The managerial merry-go-round saw Graeme Souness replaced by former Anfield 'Boot Roomer' Roy Evans, as the Reds continued in their quest for a return to former glories. Anfield said goodbye to the Kop as redevelopment work continues.
QUEENS PARK RANGERS	42	16	12	14	62	61	+1	60	With quality players of real pedigree, Rangers had been hoping for an improvement on the previous season's fifth placing in the Premiership. But it wasn't to be.
ASTON VILLA	42	15	12	15	46	50	-4	57	Ron Atkinson's Villans had an indifferent Premiership season which was enlivened by a brilliant Coca-Cola Cup Final victory over Manchester United.
COVENTRY CITY	42	14	14	14	43	45	-2	55	The Sky Blues were involved in the title run-in and effectively decided the matter in Manchester United's favour on 2 May with a 2-0 victory over second-placed Blackburn.
NORWICH CITY	42	12	17	13	65	61	+4	53	A season of highs and lows for the Canaries. They enjoyed an excellent adventure in the UEFA Cup - but the departure of manager Mike Walker heralded an anti-climax as the club settled for a mid-table berth.
WEST HAM UNITED	42	13	13	16	47	58	-11	52	After a poor start, Billy Bonds' Hammers pulled themselves together in mid-term - thanks largely to an injection of ex-Merseyside talent and the signing of wandering star Lee Chapman.
CHELSEA	42	13	12	17	49	53	-4	51	The only side to beat Manchester United twice in the Premiership. The Blues also met United for a third encounter, in the FA Cup Final, but could not prevent them from completing the 'double'. Chelsea will fly the blue flag in Europe this season in the Cup-Winners' Cup.
TOTTENHAM HOTSPUR	42	11	12	19	54	59	-5	45	A long run of poor results plunged Ossie Ardiles' Spurs into deep waters and they floundered in their worst-ever home form. Only a late swim to safety saved White Hart Lane's blushes.
MANCHESTER CITY	42	9	18	15	38	49	-11	45	Francis Lee's arrival as Chairman signalled an improvement in the Sky Blues' form - just enough to lift them out of the danger-zone.
EVERTON	42	12	8	22	42	63	-21	44	Scared the living daylights out of their fans, and only escaped the big drop in the second half of the last game of the season - a 3-2 home victory over Wimbledon. The Toffees are now enjoying their 41st season in the top flight.
SOUTHAMPTON	42	12	7	23	49	66	-17	43	Saints Preserved - but only just! They made the Great Escape in the last match of the season - a memorable 3-3 draw away to West Ham.
IPSWICH TOWN	42	9	16	17	35	58	-23	43	A battling 0-0 draw with runners-up Blackburn in the last game of the season was enough to keep the East Anglians in the Premiership.
SHEFFIELD UNITED	42	8	18	16	42	60	-18	42	Dave Bassett's Blades were almost sure of safety. They were holding Chelsea 2-2 in the last game. Then, with just 30 seconds left, Mark Stein hit the winner and United went down.
OLDHAM ATHLETIC	42	9	13	20	42	68	-26	40	Having clung on for the past two seasons, Joe Royle's luck finally ran out and the Latics were relegated. Needed a big win in the last match against Norwich, but only managed a 1-1 draw.
SWINDON TOWN	42	5	15	22	47	100	-53	30	Didn't stand a chance, despite playing attractive football. The pre-season departure of Glenn Hoddle did little to boost the Robins' confidence. And the century of goals conceded tells its own sad story.

LEEDS UNITED

Chairman: L H Silver OBE
Secretary: W J Fotherby
Team Manager: Howard Wilkinson
Sponsors: Thistle Hotels
Nickname: 'United'
Team Colours: All white with blue and yellow trim
Change Colours: Blue and yellow wide-striped shirts, blue shorts, yellow socks with blue trim
Pitch dimensions: 110 x 72yds
Ground Capacity: 41,712

PREMIERSHIP PERFORMANCE 1993 - 94

P	W	D	L	F	A	GD	Pts	Pos
42	18	16	8	65	39	+26	70	5th

Leading Scorer: Rod Wallace (17)
Average Attendance: 36,368
Highest Attendance: 41,125

Elland Road, Leeds, LS11 OES.
Telephone: 0532 716037
Fax: 0532 720370
Ticket Information: 0532 710710

Squad Stats (*Matches started - Sub played - Sub not played - Goals*):
David Batty 8-1-1-0, Mark Beeney 22-0-20-0, Brian Deane 41-0-0-11, Tony Dorigo 37-0-0-0, Chris Fairclough 40-0-1-4, Mark Ford 0-1-0-0, Jamie Forrester 2-1-2-0, Steve Hodge 7-1-6-1, Garry Kelly 42-0-0-0, John Lukic 20-0-22-0, Gary McAllister 42-0-0-8, Jon Newsome 25-4-4-1, David O'Leary 10-0-0-0, John Pemberton 6-3-4-0, David Rocastle 6-1-2-1, Kevin Sharp 7-0-1-0, Kevin R Sharp 0-3-0-0, Gary Speed 35-1-0-10, Gordon Strachan 32-1-1-3, Frank Strandli 0-4-2-0, Ray Wallace 0-1-0-0, Rod Wallace 34-3-1-17, David Wetherall 31-1-3-1, Noel Whelan 6-10-4-0, David White 9-6-2-5.

LEICESTER CITY

City Stadium, Filbert Street,
Leicester, LE2 7FL.
Telephone: 0533 555000
Fax: 0533 470585
Ticket Information: 0891 121028

HONOURS
League Cup Winners: 1964

Chairman: Martin George
Secretary: Alan Bennett
Team Manager: Brian Little
Sponsors: Walkers Crisps
Nickname: 'The Filberts'
Team Colours: All blue
Change Colours: All white
Pitch Dimensions: 112 x 75yds
Ground Capacity: 24,000

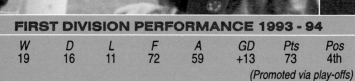

FIRST DIVISION PERFORMANCE 1993 - 94

P	W	D	L	F	A	GD	Pts	Pos
46	19	16	11	72	59	+13	73	4th

(Promoted via play-offs)

Leading Scorer: Iwan Roberts (17)
Average Attendance: 10,366
Highest Attendance: 21,744

Leicester return to the top flight in their third successive attempt in a play-off Final. The 2-1 victory over Derby was the club's first-ever victory at Wembley in seven visits there!

LIVERPOOL

Anfield Road, Liverpool, L4 OTH.
Telephone: 051-263 2361
Fax: 051-260 8813
Ticket Information: 051-260 8680
Club Shop: 051-263 1760

Chairman: D R Moores
Secretary: P B Robinson
Team Manager: Roy Evans
Sponsors: Carlsberg
Nickname: 'The Reds'
Team Colours: All red with white trim
Change Colours: White shirts with green sleeves and black trim, black shorts with white trim, black and green socks with white hoops
Pitch dimensions: 110 x 75yds
Ground Capacity: 40,000

PREMIERSHIP PERFORMANCE 1993-94

P	W	D	L	F	A	GD	Pts	Pos
42	17	9	16	59	55	+4	60	8th

Leading Scorer: Ian Rush (14)
Average Attendance: 38,503
Highest Attendance: 44,601

Squad Stats (*Matches started - Sub played - Sub not playcd - Goals*):
John Barnes 24-2-0-3, Stig Bjornebye 6-3-2-0, David Burrows 3-1-1-0, Phil Charnock 0-0-1-0, Nigel Clough 25-2-6-7, Julian Dicks 24-0-0-3, Robbie Fowler 27-1-0-12, Mark Gayle 0-0-3-0, Bruce Grobbelaar 29-0-10-0, Steve Harkness 10-1-3-0, Mike Hooper 0-0-8-0, Don Hutchison 6-5-3-0, David James 13-1-20-0, Rob Jones 38-0-0-0, Mike Marsh 0-2-1-1, Dominic Matteo 11-0-4-0, Steve McManaman 29-1-2-2, Jan Molby 11-0-1-2, Steve Nicol 27-4-4-1, Torben Piechnik 1-0-1-0, Jamie Redknapp 29-6-0-4, Ronny Rosenthal 0-3-0-0, Neil Ruddock 39-0-0-3, Ian Rush 41-1-0-14, Paul Stewart 7-1-0-0, Michael Thomas 1-6-2-0, Mark Walters 7-10-3-0, Ronnie Whelan 23-0-1-1, Mark Wright 31-0-0-1.

HONOURS

League Champions: 1900-01, 1905-06, 1921-22, 1922-23, 1946-47, 1963-64, 1965-66, 1972-73, 1975-76, 1976-77, 1978-79, 1979-80, 1981-82, 1982-83, 1983-84, 1985-86, 1987-88, 1989-90 (18)
FA Cup Winners: 1965, 1974, 1986, 1989, 1992 (5)
League Cup Winners: 1981, 1982, 1983, 1984 (4)
Charity Shield Winners: 1964 - shared, 1965 - shared, 1966, 1974, 1976, 1977 - shared, 1979, 1980, 1982, 1986 - shared, 1988, 1989, 1990 (13)
European Cup Winners: 1977, 1978, 1981, 1984 (4)
UEFA Cup Winners: 1973, 1976 (2)
European Super Cup Winners: 1977 (1)

MANCHESTER CITY

Chairman: F H Lee
Secretary: J B Halford
Team Manager: Brian Horton
Sponsors: Brother
Nickname: 'The Citizens'
Team Colours: Sky blue shirts with navy trim, white shorts with navy and sky blue trim, sky blue socks with white and navy tops
Change Colours: Purple shirts with white stripe, purple shorts, purple socks
Pitch dimensions: 117 x 75yds
Ground Capacity: 32,000

HONOURS

League Champions: 1936-37, 1967-68 (2)
FA Cup Winners: 1904, 1934, 1956, 1969 (4)
League Cup Winners: 1970, 1976 (2)
Charity Shield Winners: 1937, 1968, 1972 (3)
European Cup-Winners' Cup Winners: 1970 (1)

PREMIERSHIP PERFORMANCE 1993-94

P	W	D	L	F	A	GD	Pts	Pos
42	9	18	15	38	49	-11	45	16th

Leading Scorer:	Mike Sheron (6)
Average Attendance:	26,709
Highest Attendance:	35,115

Squad Stats (*Matches started - Sub played - Sub not played - Goals*):
Peter Beagrie 9-0-0-1, David Brightwell 19-3-6-1, Ian Brightwell 6-1-0-0, Tony Coton 31-0-2-0, Keith Curle 29-0-0-1, Andy Dibble 11-0-28-0, Richard Edghill 22-0-0-0, Steve Finney 0-0-1-0, Gary Flitcroft 19-2-1-3, John Foster 1-0-0-0, Carl Griffith 11-5-2-4, Alfons Groenendijk 9-0-0-0, Andy Hill 15-2-0-0, Rick Holden 9-0-0-0, Kaare Ingebrigtsen 2-5-1-0, Rae Ingram 0-0-1-0, Steffen Karl 4-2-3-1, Alan Kernaghan 23-1-0-0, David Kerr 2-0-0-0, Steve Lomas 17-6-6-0, Martyn Margetson 0-0-12-0, Steve McMahon 35-0-0-0, Adrian Mike 1-8-2-1, Terry Phelan 30-0-1-1, Mike Quigley 2-0-4-0, Niall Quinn 14-1-0-5, Peter Reid 1-3-0-0, David Rocastle 21-0-0-2, Uwe Rosler 12-0-0-5, Mike Sheron 29-4-3-6, Carl Shutt 5-1-1-0, Fitzroy Simpson 12-3-2-0, Mike Vonk 34-1-2-1, Paul Walsh 11-0-0-4, David White 16-0-0-1.

Maine Road, Moss Side, Manchester, M14 7WN.
Telephone: 061-226 1191/2
Fax: 061-227 9418
Ticket Information: 061-226 2224

THE GOALGETTERS

Newcastle's Andy Cole topped the Premiership's goalscoring chart with 34 superstrikes. Meanwhile, he also became the first-ever Newcastle player to score more than 40 League and Cup goals in a season. In all, Andy hit 41 goals in the Premiership, the FA Cup and the Coca-Cola Cup.

MOST CLEAN SHEETS

David Seaman	Arsenal	20
Peter Schmeichel	Manchester United	15
Ludek Miklosko	West Ham United	14
Tim Flowers	Blackburn Rovers	13

Above: Ian Wright - 23 goals

Left: Chris Sutton - 25 goals

THE PREMIERSHIP'S TOP TEN MARKSMEN 1993-94

1	Andy Cole	Newcastle United	34
2	Alan Shearer	Blackburn Rovers	31
3	Chris Sutton	Norwich City	25
3	Matthew Le Tissier	Southampton	25
5	Ian Wright	Arsenal	23
6	Peter Beardsley	Newcastle United	21
7	Mark Bright	Sheffield Wednesday	19
8	Eric Cantona	Manchester United	18
9	Rod Wallace	Leeds United	17
9	Dean Holdsworth	Wimbledon	17

Matthew Le Tissier -
25 goals

Alan Shearer - 31 goals

MOST GOALS IN A GAME
4 **Efan Ekoku** for Norwich City v Everton

FASTEST GOAL
26 seconds **Matthew Le Tissier** for Southampton v Liverpool

Rod Wallace - 17 goals

PENALTY KINGS

Peter Beardsley	Newcastle United	7
Matthew Le Tissier	Southampton	6
Paul Bodin	Swindon Town	5
Ian Wright	Arsenal	5
Teddy Sheringham	Tottenham Hotspur	4

Mark Bright - 19 goals

Andy Cole - 34 goals

the Men In Green

Love 'em or hate 'em, the Premierships referees play a vital role all season long. Without them, we'd never get through a season! Our cameras have been focussing on...

It isn't only players who need talking too!

Inset: That's blown it - Phil Don in action

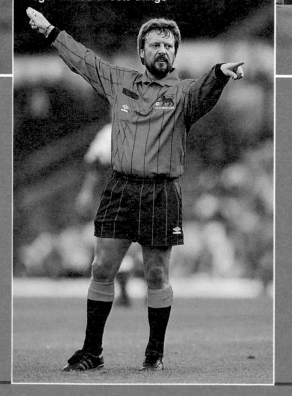
Roger Dilkes directs things

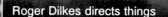
'Calm down, calm down,' says Paul Durkin

MANCHESTER UNITED

Sir Matt Busby Way, Old Trafford,
Manchester, M16 ORA.
Telephone: 061-872 1661
Fax: 061-876 5502
Ticket Information: 061-872 0199

HONOURS

League Champions: 1907-08,
1910-11, 1951-52, 1955-56,
1956-57, 1964-65, 1966-67,
1992-93, 1993-94 (9)
FA Cup Winners: 1909, 1948, 1963,
1977, 1983, 1985, 1990, 1994 (8)
League Cup Winners: 1992 (1)
Charity Shield Winners: 1908,
1911, 1952, 1956, 1957, 1965 -
shared, 1967 - shared, 1977 -
shared, 1983, 1993 (10)
European Cup Winners: 1968 (1)
*European Cup-Winners' Cup
Winners:* 1991 (1)
European Super Cup Winners:
1991 (1)

PREMIERSHIP PERFORMANCE 1993-94

P	W	D	L	F	A	GD	Pts	Pos
42	27	11	4	80	38	+42	92	1st

Leading Scorer: Eric Cantona (18)
Average Attendance: 44,244
Highest Attendance: 44,751

Squad Stats (*Matches started - Sub played - Sub not played - Goals*):
Steve Bruce 41-0-0-3, Nicky Butt 0-1-1-0, Eric Cantona 34-0-0-18, Dion Dublin 1-4-5-1,
Darren Ferguson 1-2-4-0, Ryan Giggs 32-6-2-13, Mark Hughes 36-0-0-12, Paul Ince
39-0-0-8, Denis Irwin 42-0-0-2, Andrei Kanchelskis 28-3-4-6, Roy Keane 34-3-0-5, Lee
Martin 1-0-1-0, Brian McClair 12-14-10-1, Colin McKee 1-0-0-0, Gary Neville 1-0-0-0,
Gary Pallister 41-0-0-1, Paul Parker 39-1-0-0, Mike Phelan 1-1-2-0, Bryan Robson 10-
5-9-1, Peter Schmeichel 40-0-0-0, Les Sealey 0-0-39-0, Lee Sharpe 26-4-2-9, Ben
Thornley 0-1-0-0, Gary Walsh 2-1-2-0.

Chairman/Chief Executive:
C M Edwards
Secretary: K R Merrett
Team Manager: Alex Ferguson
Sponsors: Sharp Electronics
Nickname: 'The Red Devils'
Team Colours: Red shirts, white
shorts, black socks
Change Colours: All black
Pitch dimensions: 116 x 76yds
Ground Capacity: 44,000

MANCHESTER UN
PREMIERSHIP

MANCHESTER UNITED LED THE TITLE CHASE ALMOST FROM THE FIRST KICK-OFF OF THE SEASON. THEY FINISHED THE CAMPAIGN WITH A PREMIERSHIP RECORD OF 92 POINTS - EIGHT MORE THAN THEY AMASSED IN WINNING THE 1992-93 CHAMPIONSHIP. AND, OF COURSE, THEY WENT ON TO COMPLETE A HISTORY-MAKING SEASON BY BEATING CHELSEA 4-0 IN THE FA CUP FINAL AND BECOMING ONLY THE SIXTH CLUB IN ENGLISH SOCCER HISTORY TO COMPLETE THE 'DOUBLE'...

A happy squad: United show off the Premiership trophy

ITED - THE 1993-94 CHAMPIONS

It's party time at Old Trafford!

Right: Ryan Giggs
lifts the trophy

NEWCASTLE UNITED

St James' Park, Newcastle-upon-Tyne, NE1 4ST.
Telephone: 091-232 8361
Fax: 091-232 9875
Ticket Information: 091-261 1571

Chairman: Sir John Hall
Secretary: F Fletcher
Team Manager: Kevin Keegan
Sponsors: Newcastle Breweries
Nickname: 'The Magpies'
Team Colours: Black and white striped shirts, black shorts, black socks and white trim
Change Colours: All blue with black turnover on socks
Pitch dimensions: 110 x 73yds
Ground Capacity: 37,000

PREMIERSHIP PERFORMANCE 1993-94

P	W	D	L	F	A	GD	Pts	Pos
42	23	8	11	82	41	+41	77	3rd

Leading Scorer:	Andy Cole (34)
Average Attendance:	33,792
Highest Attendance:	36,388

Squad Stats (*Matches started - Sub played - Sub not played - Goals*):
Malcolm Allen 9-0-5-5, Matthew Appleby 1-0-3-0, Peter Beardsley 35-0-0-21, John Beresford 34-0-0-0, Paul Bracewell 32-0-0-1, John Burridge 0-0-2-0, Lee Clark 29-0-0-2, Andy Cole 40-0-0-34, Robert Elliott 13-2-2-0, Ruel Fox 14-0-0-2, Chris Holland 2-1-0-0, Mike Hooper 19-0-15-0, Steve Howey 13-1-0-0, Mike Jeffrey 2-0-1-0, Brian Kilcline 1-0-8-0, Robert Lee 41-0-0-7, Alex Mathie 0-16-13-3, Alan Neilson 10-4-5-0, Liam O'Brien 4-2-3-0, Nico Papavassiliou 7-0-0-0, Darren Peacock 9-0-0-0, Brian Reid 0-0-1-0, Mark Robinson 12-4-2-0, Kevin Scott 18-0-2-0, Scott Sellars 29-1-2-3, Pavel Srnicek 21-0-20-0, Barry Venison 36-1-0-0, Steve Watson 29-3-2-2, Tommy Wright 2-1-4-0.

HONOURS
League Champions: 1904-05, 1906-07, 1908-09, 1926-27 (4)
FA Cup Winners: 1910, 1924, 1932, 1951, 1952, 1955 (6)
Charity Shield Winners: 1909 (1)
UEFA Cup Winners: 1969 (1)

NORWICH CITY

HONOURS
League Cup Winners: 1962, 1985 (2)

Carrow Road, Norwich, NR1 1JE.
Telephone: 0603 760760
Fax: 0603 665510
Ticket Information: 0603 761661
Club Shop: 0603 761125

PREMIERSHIP PERFORMANCE 1993-94

P	W	D	L	F	A	GD	Pts	Pos
42	12	17	13	65	61	+4	53	12th

Leading Scorer:	Chris Sutton (25)
Average Attendance:	18,179
Highest Attendance:	21,181

Squad Stats (*Matches started - Sub played - Sub not played - Goals*):
Neil Adams 11-3-0-0, Adeola Akinbiyi 0-2-1-0, Mark Bowen 41-0-0-5, Ian Butterworth 23-2-3-0, Ian Crook 38-0-0-0, Ian Culverhouse 42-0-0-1, Darren Eadie 9-6-4-3, Efan Ekoku 20-7-2-12, Ruel Fox 25-0-0-7, Jeremy Goss 34-0-0-6, Bryan Gunn 41-0-0-0, Scott Howie 1-1-39-0, Andy Johnson 0-2-4-0, Andy Marshall 0-0-2-0, Gary Megson 21-1-8-0, Rob Newman 32-0-0-2, John Polston 24-0-1-0, Lee Power 2-3-0-0, Spencer Prior 13-0-2-0, Mark Robins 9-4-4-1, David Smith 5-2-9-0, Daryl Sutch 1-2-0-0, Chris Sutton 41-0-0-25, Robert Ullathorne 11-5-6-2, Colin Woodthorpe 18-2-2-0.

Chairman: R T Chase
Secretary: A R W Neville
Team Manager: John Deehan
Sponsors: Norwich & Peterborough Building Society
Nickname: 'The Canaries'
Team Colours: Yellow shirts, green shorts, yellow socks
Change Colours: All white with blackcurrant trim
Pitch dimensions: 114 x 74yds
Ground Capacity: 22,000

31

NOTTINGHAM FOREST

City Ground, Nottingham, NG2 5FJ.
Telephone: 0602 822202
Fax: 0602 455581
Ticket Information: 0602 813801
Club Shop: 0602 822664

Chairman: F Reacher
Secretary: P White
Team Manager: Frank Clark
Sponsors: Labatt's
Nickname: 'Forest'
Team Colours: Red shirts, white shorts, red socks
Change Colours: White shirts, black shorts, white socks
Pitch Dimensions: 115 x 78yds
Ground Capacity: 28,264

1ST DIVISION PERFORMANCE 1993-94

P	W	D	L	F	A	GD	Pts	Pos
46	23	14	9	74	49	+25	83	2nd

Leading Scorer: Stan Collymore (19)
Average Attendance: 23,051
Highest Attendance: 27,010

Frank Clark led Forest's return to the top flight at the first time of asking, as runners-up to Crystal Palace in the '93-94 First Division race.

HONOURS

League Champions: 1977-78 (1)
FA Cup Winners: 1898, 1959 (2)
League Cup Winners: 1978, 1979, 1989, 1990 (4)
European Cup Winners: 1979, 1980 (2)
European Super Cup Winners: 1980 (1)

QUEENS PARK RANGERS

Rangers Stadium, South Africa
Road, London, W12 7PA.
Telephone: 081-743 0262
Fax: 081-749 0994
Ticket Information: 081-749 5744
Club Shop: 081-749 6862

Chairman: R C Thompson
Secretary: S F Marson
Team Manager: Gerry Francis
Sponsors: Compaq
Nickname: 'Rangers'
Team Colours: Blue and white hooped shirts, white shorts, white socks
Change Colours: All black with red trim
Pitch Dimensions: 112 x 72yds
Ground Capacity: 20,000

PREMIERSHIP PERFORMANCE 1993-94

P	W	D	L	F	A	GD	Pts	Pos
42	16	12	14	62	61	+1	60	9th

Leading Scorer: Les Ferdinand (16)
Average Attendance: 14,113
Highest Attendance: 21,267

Squad Stats (*Matches started - Sub played - Sub not played - Goals*):
Bradley Allen 14-7-3-7, Dennis Bailey 0-0-2-0, David Bardsley 32-0-0-0, Simon Barker 35-2-0-5, Rufus Brevett 3-4-15-0, Maurice Doyle 1-0-0-0, Les Ferdinand 35-1-0-16, Ian Holloway 19-6-1-0, Andrew Impey 31-1-3-3, Danny Maddix 0-0-2-0, Alan McCarthy 4-0-1-0, Alan McDonald 12-0-1-1, Mike Meaker 11-3-0-1, Darren Peacock 30-0-0-3, Gary Penrice 23-3-1-8, Karl Ready 19-3-5-1, Tony Roberts 16-0-26-0, Trevor Sinclair 30-2-0-4, Jan Stejskal 26-0-16-0, Devon White 12-6-4-7, Ray Wilkins 39-0-1-1, Clive Wilson 42-0-0-3, Tony Witter 1-0-1-0, Steve Yates 27-2-4-0.

HONOURS
League Cup Winners: 1967 (1)

Gary McAllister - Mr Consistency

Goalgetting Don, Dean Holdsworth

THE FUTURE OF THE PREMIERSHIP LOOKS BRIGHT AND CLEAR, ESPECIALLY WITH PLAYERS LIKE THESE AROUND...

PREMIERSHIP STARS OF '93-94

The Football Writers' Association 'Footballer of the Year Award' for 1994 was presented to ALAN SHEARER. A prodigious striker with 31 Premiership goals for Blackburn Rovers, Alan also made quite an impact on Terry Venables's revitalised England side.

The members of The Professional Footballers' Association voted ERIC CANTONA their 'Player of the Year'. Even in a season tinged with personal controversy, the mercurial Frenchman stood out in Manchester United's team of superstars and became the first foreign player to receive the PFA's prestigious award.

Forty-one goal ANDY COLE took the PFA's 'Young Player of the Year' award. With the Newcastle United superstriker AND Alan Shearer around, England's prospects in the next European Championship are looking increasingly healthy.

Other players who made an impact in 1993-94 included PETER BEARDSLEY, who has proved that advancing years mean little when it comes to quality football. His magical performances for Newcastle caught the eye of England boss Terry Venables and his return to the international arena added a touch of class to the side.

MATTHEW LE TISSIER was another player who returned to the headlines in 1993-94. His scintillating performances and stunning goals for Southampton were instrumental in keeping the club in the Premiership.

GARY McALLISTER was a model of consistency throughout the season for Leeds United, while Tottenham's DARREN ANDERTON was an outstanding player in a relatively poor campaign for his club. Darren's valiant efforts were also rewarded with a place in Terry Venables' England set-up.

Between December and February Chelsea's MARK STEIN notched a notable record for himself by scoring ten goals in seven consecutive Premiership matches. Another terrific goalscorer with a fine future ahead of him was DEAN HOLDSWORTH of Wimbledon.

At the other end of the pitch DAVID SEAMAN had a fine season, keeping twenty clean sheets as Arsenal conceded less goals than any other Premiership side.

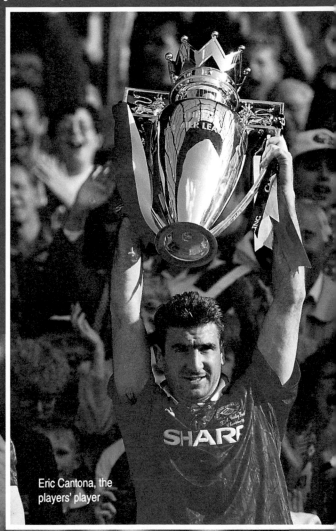

Eric Cantona, the players' player

Peter Beardsley, quality player

35

SHEFFIELD WEDNESDAY

Hillsborough, Sheffield, S6 1SW.
Telephone: 0742 343122
Fax: 0742 337145
Ticket Information: 0742 337233
Club Shop: 0742 343342

Chairman: D G Richards
Secretary: G H Mackrell
Team Manager: Trevor Francis
Sponsors: Sanderson Electronics
Nickname: 'The Owls'
Team Colours: Blue and white striped shirts, blue shorts, blue and white socks
Change Colours: All black with yellow trim
Pitch Dimensions: 115 x 75yds
Ground Capacity: 32,000

PREMIERSHIP PERFORMANCE 1993-94

P	W	D	L	F	A	GD	Pts	Pos
42	16	16	10	76	54	+22	64	7th

Leading Scorer: Mark Bright (19)
Average Attendance: 27,187
Highest Attendance: 34,959

Squad Stats (*Matches started - Sub played - Sub not played - Goals*):
Chris Bart-Williams 30-7-1-8, Mark Bright 36-4-0-19, Lee Briscoe 0-1-0-0, Simon Coleman 10-5-0-1, Trevor Francis 0-1-0-0, David Hirst 6-1-0-1, Graham Hyde 27-9-0-1, Nigel Jemson 10-8-7-5, Ryan Jones 24-2-2-6, Lance Key 0-0-10-0, Phil King 7-3-0-0, Brian Linighan 1-0-1-0, Roland Nilsson 38-0-0-0, Carlton Palmer 37-0-0-5, Andy Pearce 29-3-3-3, Nigel Pearson 4-1-0-0, Adem Poric 2-4-6-0, Kevin Pressman 32-0-10-0, John Sheridan 19-1-0-3, Andy Sinton 25-0-0-3, Chris Waddle 19-0-0-3, Des Walker 42-0-0-0, Paul Warhurst 4-0-0-0, Gordon Watson 15-8-3-12, Julian Watts, 1-0-0-0, Mike Williams 4-0-2-0, Chris Woods 10-0-22-0, Nigel Worthington 30-0-1-1.

HONOURS

League Champions: 1902-03, 1903-04, 1928-29, 1929-30 (4)
FA Cup Winners: 1896, 1907, 1935 (3)
League Cup Winners: 1991 (1)
Charity Shield Winners: 1935 (1)

SOUTHAMPTON

The Dell, Milton Road,
Southampton, SO9 4XX.
Telephone: 0703 220505
Fax: 0703 330360
Ticket Information: 0703 228575

Chairman: F G L Askham
Secretary: B P Truscott
Team Manager: Alan Ball
Sponsors: Dimplex
Nickname: 'The Saints'
Team Colours: Red and white striped shirts, black shorts, black socks with red and white trim
Change Colours: Turquoise shirts with royal blue stripe, turquoise shorts, royal blue socks with turquoise trim
Pitch Dimensions: 110 x 72yds
Ground Capacity: 19,200

PREMIERSHIP PERFORMANCE 1993-94

P	W	D	L	F	A	GD	Pts	Pos
42	12	7	23	49	66	-17	43	18th

Leading Scorer: Matthew Le Tissier (25)
Average Attendance: 14,764
Highest Attendance: 19,105

Squad Stats (*Matches started - Sub played - Sub not played - Goals*):
Micky Adams 17-2-1-0, Paul Allen 29-3-3-1, Ian Andrews 5-0-37-0, Nicky Banger 4-10-2-0, Neal Bartlett 4-3-1-0, Dave Beasant 25-0-4-0, Francis Benali 34-3-2-0, Frank Bennett 0-8-7-1, Matthew Bound 1-0-3-0, Simon Charlton 29-4-1-1, Glenn Cockerill 12-2-0-0, Colin Cramb 0-1-0-0, Jason Dodd 5-5-4-0, Iain Dowie 39-0-0-5, Tim Flowers 12-0-0-0, Richard Hall 4-0-0-0, Neil Heaney 2-0-0-0, Neil Hopper 0-0-1-0, David Hughes 0-2-1-0, Terry Hurlock 2-0-1-0, Jeff Kenna 40-0-1-2, Matthew Le Tissier 38-0-0-25, Neil Maddison 41-0-0-7, Jim Magilton 15-0-0-0, Craig Maskell 6-4-3-1, Ken Monkou 35-0-0-4, Paul Moody 3-2-0-0, Kevin Moore 14-0-3-0, Lee Powell 1-0-0-0, Peter Reid 7-0-0-0, Tommy Widdrington 11-0-2-1, Steve Wood 27-0-0-0.

HONOURS
FA Cup Winners: 1976 (1)

TOTTENHAM HOTSPUR

Chairman: A M Sugar
Secretary: P R Barnes
Team Manager: Ossie Ardiles
Sponsors: Holsten
Nickname: 'Spurs'
Team Colours: White shirts, navy shorts, white socks
Change Colours: All sky blue
Pitch Dimensions: 110 x 73yds
Ground Capacity: 31,550

748 High Road, Tottenham, London, N17 OAP.
Telephone: 081-365 5000
Fax: 081-365 5005
Ticket Information: 081-808 8080

PREMIERSHIP PERFORMANCE 1993-94

P	W	D	L	F	A	GD	Pts	Pos
42	11	12	19	54	59	-5	45	15th

Leading Scorer:	Teddy Sheringham (14)
Average Attendance:	27,255
Highest Attendance:	33,130

Squad Stats (*Matches started - Sub played - Sub not played - Goals*):
Paul Allen 0-1-0-0, Darren Anderton 35-2-1-6, Dean Austin 20-3-6-0, Nick Barmby 27-0-0-5, Colin Calderwood 26-0-0-0, Sol Campbell 27-7-5-0, Steve Carr 1-0-0-0, Darren Caskey 16-9-3-4, Chris Day 0-0-7-0, Jason Dozzell 28-4-0-8, Gordon Durie 10-0-0-1, Justin Edinburgh 24-1-0-0, Andy Gray 0-2-3-1, Mike Hazard 13-4-0-2, John Hendry 0-3-4-0, Danny Hill 1-2-0-0, David Howells 15-3-1-1, David Kerslake 16-1-1-0, Gary Mabbutt 29-0-0-0, Paul Mahorn 1-0-0-0, Paul Moran 0-5-3-0, Stuart Nethercott 9-1-1-0, Steve Robinson 1-1-0-0, Ronny Rosenthal 11-4-0-2, Vinny Samways 39-0-0-3, Kevin Scott 12-0-0-1, Steve Sedgley 42-0-0-5, Teddy Sheringham 17-2-0-14, Erik Thorstvedt 32-0-3-0, Andy Turner 0-1-0-0, Ian Walker 10-1-31-0.

HONOURS

League Champions: 1950-51, 1960-61 (2)
FA Cup Winners: 1901, 1921, 1961, 1962, 1967, 1981, 1982, 1991 (8)
League Cup Winners: 1971, 1973 (2)
Charity Shield Winners: 1920, 1951, 1961, 1962, 1967 - shared, 1991 - shared (6)
European Cup-Winners' Cup Winners: 1963 (1)
UEFA Cup Winners: 1972, 1984 (2)

WEST HAM UNITED

Boleyn Ground, Green Street,
Upton Park, London, E13 9AZ.
Telephone: 081-548 2748
Fax: 081-548 2758
Ticket Information: 081-472 3322

HONOURS
FA Cup Winners: 1964, 1975, 1980
(3)
Charity Shield Winners: 1964 -
shared (1)
*European Cup-Winners' Cup
Winners:* 1965 (1)

PREMIERSHIP PERFORMANCE 1993-94

P	W	D	L	F	A	GD	Pts	Pos
42	13	13	16	47	58	-11	52	13th

Leading Scorer: Trevor Morley (13)
Average Attendance: 20,595
Highest Attendance: 28,832

Chairman: T W Brown
Secretary: T M Finn
Team Manager: Billy Bonds
Sponsors: Dagenham Motors
Nickname: 'The Hammers'
Team Colours: Claret shirts with
blue sleeves, white shorts, white
socks with claret and blue trim
Change Colours: Blue shirts with
two claret hoops, blue shorts, blue
socks
Pitch Dimensions: 112 x 72yds
Ground Capacity: 30,000

Squad Stats (*Matches started - Sub played - Sub not played - Goals*):
Clive Allen 7-0-2-2, Martin Allen 20-6-4-7, Ian Bishop 36-0-0-1, Jeroen Boere 0-4-5-0, Tim Breacker 40-0-0-3, Kenny Brown 6-3-6-0, Alex Bunbury 0-0-1-0, David Burrows 25-0-0-1, Peter Butler 26-0-0-1, Lee Chapman 26-4-2-8, Julian Dicks 7-0-0-0, Colin Foster 5-0-0-0, Tony Gale 31-1-4-0, Dale Gordon 8-0-1-1, Matt Holmes 33-1-1-3, Steve Jones 3-5-8-2, Gary Kelly 0-0-15-0, Paul Marquis 0-1-0-0, Mike Marsh 33-0-0-1, Alvin Martin 6-1-0-2, Ludek Miklosko 42-0-0-0, Paul Mitchell 0-1-1-0, Trevor Morley 39-3-0-13 Martin Peat 0-0-1-0, Gerry Peyton 0-0-26-0, Steve Potts 41-0-0-0, Mark Robson 1-2-1-0, Keith Rowland 16-7-6-0, Matthew Rush 9-1-1-1, Danny Williamson 2-1-0-1.

UPS and DOWNS

The relegation was every bit as exciting and dramatic as the race for the title.

Throughout 1993-94 bottom place in the Premiership belonged to Swindon Town. In the top flight for the first time, they never really got going and managed only five victories all season.

Swindon were eventually joined in the big drop by Oldham and Sheffield United - both clubs' fates were sealed in

The shirt says it all as Crystal Palace celebrate their return to the top flight

their last games of the season.

The First Division campaign saw the immediate return of two of the clubs relegated in 1992-93. Crystal Palace performed brilliantly all season to emerge as Champions, while Nottingham Forest succeeded in their late bid for an automatic promotion place.

The First Division play-offs, to decide who would accompany Palace and Forest into the Premiership, were contested by Millwall, Leicester City, Tranmere Rovers and Derby County.

After the two-legged preliminary knock-out round, Derby met Leicester in the play-off Final at Wembley on Monday 30 May. County were hoping for a return to the top flight after a three year absence. City, who had been relegated in 1986-87, were contesting their third play-off Final at Wembley - indeed the club had played in the famous stadium six times in all and had yet to win there.

The match was played in blazing sunshine and the two teams produced an exciting game in front of a 73,671 crowd. The Rams struck first, on 27 minutes, when Tommy Johnson latched onto a superb through ball from Paul Simpson. The

The Palace crowd celebrate too!

Leicester's Steve Walsh (No.9) gets the equaliser against Derby County in the play-off Final at Wembley

striker's pace took him through the Leicester defence and he fired home a terrific left-foot shot.

Leicester clawed their way back into the game and four minutes before half-time they were back on level terms when a high and hopeful ball was not cleared by the Derby defence. Steve Walsh grabbed the golden opportunity to equalise.

In the 84th minute Derby's USA international John Harkes fluffed a clear chance with only the keeper to beat. A minute after that, the tables were turned completely when Steve Walsh whacked home a rebounding cross to give Leicester a 2-1 lead.

The last five minutes were hectic with both sides going close, but Leicester held on to fill the final place in the 1994-95 Premiership contest.

Steve Walsh's 85th minute goal took Leicester City into the Premiership

Celebration time for the lads from Leicester

41

SOCCER RECORDS

YEAR	CHAMPIONS	YEAR	CHAMPIONS	YEAR	CHAMPIONS
1888-89	Preston North End	1914-15	Everton	1970-71	Arsenal
1889-90	Preston North End	1919-20	West Bromwich Albion	1971-72	Derby
1890-91	Everton	1920-21	Burnley	1972-73	Liverpool
1891-92	Sunderland	1921-22	Liverpool	1973-74	Leeds United
1892-93	Sunderland	1922-23	Liverpool	1974-75	Derby County
1893-94	Aston Villa	1923-24	Huddersfield Town	1975-76	Liverpool
1894-95	Sunderland	1924-25	Huddersfield Town	1976-77	Liverpool
1895-96	Aston Villa	1925-26	Huddersfield Town	1977-78	Nottingham Forest
1896-97	Aston Villa	1926-27	Newcastle United	1978-79	Liverpool
1897-98	Sheffield United	1927-28	Everton		
1898-99	Aston Villa	1928-29	Sheffield Wednesday		
1899-1900	Aston Villa	1929-30	Sheffield Wednesday		
1900-01	Liverpool	1930-31	Arsenal		
1901-02	Sunderland	1931-32	Everton		
1902-03	The Wednesday	1932-33	Arsenal		
1903-04	The Wednesday	1933-34	Arsenal		
1904-05	Newcastle United	1934-35	Arsenal		
1905-06	Liverpool	1935-36	Sunderland		
1906-07	Newcastle United	1936-37	Manchester City		
1907-08	Manchester United	1937-38	Arsenal		
1908-09	Newcastle United	1938-39	Everton		
1909-10	Aston Villa	1946-47	Liverpool		
1910-11	Manchester United	1947-48	Arsenal		
1911-12	Blackburn Rovers	1948-49	Portsmouth		
1912-13	Sunderland	1949-50	Portsmouth		
1913-14	Blackburn Rovers	1950-51	Tottenham Hotspur		
		1951-52	Manchester United		
		1952-53	Arsenal		
		1953-54	Wolverhampton Wanderers		
		1954-55	Chelsea		
		1955-56	Manchester United		
		1956-57	Manchester United	1979-80	Liverpool
		1957-58	Wolverhampton Wanderers	1980-81	Aston Villa
		1958-59	Wolverhampton Wanderers	1981-82	Liverpool
		1959-60	Burnley	1982-83	Liverpool
		1960-61	Tottenham Hotspur	1983-84	Liverpool
		1961-62	Ipswich Town	1984-85	Everton
		1962-63	Everton	1985-86	Liverpool
		1963-64	Liverpool	1986-87	Everton
		1964-65	Manchester United	1987-88	Liverpool
		1965-66	Liverpool	1988-89	Arsenal
		1966-67	Manchester United	1989-90	Liverpool
		1967-68	Manchester City	1990-91	Arsenal
		1968-69	Leeds United	1991-92	Leeds United
		1969-70	Everton		

PREMIER LEAGUE

YEAR	CHAMPIONS
1992-93	Manchester United
1993-94	Manchester United

The old League Championship trophy

The F.A. Carling Premiership trophy

YEAR	FA CUP WINNERS	YEAR	FA CUP WINNERS	YEAR	FA CUP WINNERS
1872	Wanderers	1889-90	Blackburn Rovers	1948-49	Wolverhampton Wanderers
1873	Wanderers	1890-91	Blackburn Rovers	1949-50	Arsenal
1874	Oxford University	1891-92	West Bromwich Albion	1950-51	Newcastle United
1875	Royal Engineers	1892-93	Wolverhampton Wanderers	1951-52	Newcastle United
1876	Wanderers	1893-94	Notts County	1952-53	Blackpool
1877	Wanderers	1894-95	Aston Villa	1953-54	West Bromwich Albion
1878	Wanderers	1895-96	Sheffield Wednesday	1954-55	Newcastle United
1879	Old Etonians	1896-97	Aston Villa	1955-56	Manchester City
1880	Clapham Rovers	1897-98	Nottingham Forest	1956-57	Aston Villa
		1898-99	Sheffield United	1957-58	Bolton Wanderers
		1899-1900	Bury	1958-59	Nottingham Forest
		1900-01	Tottenham Hotspur	1959-60	Wolverhampton Wanderers
		1901-02	Sheffield United	1960-61	Tottenham Hotspur
		1902-03	Bury	1961-62	Tottenham Hotspur
		1903-04	Manchester City	1962-63	Manchester United
		1904-05	Aston Villa	1963-64	West Ham United
		1905-06	Everton	1964-65	Liverpool
		1906-07	Sheffield Wednesday	1965-66	Everton
		1907-08	Wolverhampton Wanderers	1966-67	Tottenham Hotspur
		1908-09	Manchester United	1967-68	West Bromwich Albion
		1909-10	Newcastle United	1968-69	Manchester City
		1910-11	Bradford City	1969-70	Chelsea
		1911-12	Barnsley	1970-71	Arsenal
		1912-13	Aston Villa	1971-72	Leeds United
		1913-14	Burnley	1972-73	Sunderland
		1914-15	Sheffield United	1973-74	Liverpool
		1919-20	Aston Villa	1974-75	West Ham United
		1920-21	Tottenham Hotspur	1975-76	Southampton
		1921-22	Huddersfield Town	1976-77	Manchester United
		1922-23	Bolton Wanderers	1977-78	Ipswich Town
		1923-24	Newcastle United	1978-79	Arsenal
		1924-25	Sheffield United	1979-80	West Ham United
		1925-26	Bolton Wanderers	1980-81	Tottenham Hotspur
		1926-27	Cardiff City	1981-82	Tottenham Hotspur
		1927-28	Blackburn Rovers	1982-83	Manchester United
		1928-29	Bolton Wanderers	1983-84	Everton
		1929-30	Arsenal	1984-85	Manchester United
		1930-31	West Bromwich Albion	1985-86	Liverpool
		1931-32	Newcastle United	1986-87	Coventry City
		1932-33	Everton	1987-88	Wimbledon
1881	Old Carthusians	1933-34	Manchester City	1988-89	Liverpool
1882	Old Etonians	1934-35	Sheffield Wednesday	1989-90	Manchester United
1883	Blackburn Olympic	1935-36	Arsenal	1990-91	Tottenham Hotspur
1884	Blackburn Rovers	1936-37	Sunderland	1991-92	Liverpool
1885	Blackburn Rovers	1937-38	Preston North End	1992-93	Arsenal
1886	Blackburn Rovers	1938-39	Portsmouth	1993-94	Manchester United
1887	Aston Villa	1946	Derby County		
1888	West Bromich Albion	1946-47	Charlton Athletic		
1888-89	Preston North End	1947-48	Manchester United		

The FA Cup

YEAR	LEAGUE CUP WINNERS	YEAR	LEAGUE CUP WINNERS
1960-61	Aston Villa	1977-78	Nottingham Forest
1961-62	Norwich City	1978-79	Nottingham Forest
1962-63	Birmingham City	1979-80	Wolverhampton Wanders
1963-64	Leicester City	1980-81	Liverpool
1964-65	Chelsea	1981-82	Liverpool
1965-66	West Bromwich Albion	1982-83	Liverpool
1966-67	QPR	1983-84	Liverpool
1967-68	Leeds United	1984-85	Norwich City
1968-69	Swindon Town	1985-86	Oxford United
1969-70	Manchester City	1986-87	Arsenal
1970-71	Tottenham Hotspur	1987-88	Luton Town
1971-72	Stoke City	1988-89	Nottingham Forest
1972-73	Tottenham Hotspur	1989-90	Nottingham Forest
1973-74	Wolverhampton Wanders	1990-91	Sheffield Wednesday
1974-75	Aston Villa	1991-92	Manchester United
1975-76	Manchester City	1992-93	Arsenal
1976-77	Aston Villa	1993-94	Aston Villa

The League Cup

WIMBLEDON

Selhurst Park Ground, London,
SE25 6PY.
Telephone: 081-771 2233
Fax: 081-768 0640
Ticket Information: 081-771 8841

PREMIERSHIP PERFORMANCE 1993-94

P	W	D	L	F	A	GD	Pts	Pos
42	18	11	13	56	53	+3	65	6th

Leading Scorer: Dean Holdsworth (17)
Average Attendance: 10,462
Highest Attendance: 28,553

Squad Stats (*Matches started - Sub played - Sub not played - Goals*):
Neal Ardley 14-2-1-1, Warren Barton 37-2-1-2, Greg Berry 4-0-1-1, Dean Blackwell 16-2-5-0, Gary Blissett 6-12-7-3, Stewart Castledine 3-0-0-1, Andy Clarke 9-14-8-2, Perry Digweed 0-0-15-0, Gerry Dobbs 3-7-1-0, Robbie Earle 42-0-0-9, Gary Elkins 18-0-0-1, John Fashanu 35-1-0-11, Peter Fear 23-0-1-1, Scott Fitzgerald 27-1-1-0, Marcus Gayle 10-0-0-0, Dean Holdsworth 42-0-0-17, Vinny Jones 33-0-0-2, Roger Joseph 13-0-0-0, Alan Kimble 14-0-0-0, Brian McAllister 13-0-1-0, Paul Miller 0-0-1-0, Chris Perry 0-2-9-0, Lawrie Sanchez 15-0-0-2, John Scales 37-0-0-0, Hans Segers 41-0-1-0, Neil Sullivan 1-1-25-0, Steve Talboys 6-1-3-0.

HONOURS
FA Cup Winners: 1988 (1)

Chairman: S G Reed
Secretary: S A Rooke
Team Manager: Joe Kinnear
Sponsors: Elonex
Nickname: 'The Dons'
Team Colours: All navy blue with yellow trim
Change Colours: All red with black trim
Pitch Dimensions: 110 x 74yds
Ground Capacity: 27,119

EXCLUSIVE COMPETITION!!
WIN A
MITRE DELTA FOOTBALL -

THE OFFICIAL FOOTBALL OF THE PREMIER LEAGUE AND YOUR FOOTBALLING HEROES!

We've also got second and third prizes from Citizen and Lucozade - official suppliers of the Premier League.

ALL YOU HAVE TO DO IS ANSWER THIS HAT-TRICK OF SIMPLE QUESTIONS:

1. Which club finished as runner-up to Manchester United in the 1993-94 Premiership?

2. Who was the Premiership's leading goalscorer in 1993-94?

3. Who was Chelsea's player-manager in the 1993-94 Premiership campaign?

Send you completed entry form to:
Premier League Competition,
Grandreams,
Jadwin House, 205/211 Kentish Town Road,
London NW5 2JU.
Closing date for entries is 28th February, 1995.

First prize of the Mitre Delta football will go to the first correct entry out of the bag, the second and third correct entries will receive Citizen and Lucozade prizes. The decision of the publishers is final.

Peter Schmeichel reaches for that prize ball!

PREMIER LEAGUE COMPETITION

Answers are as follows:

1._____

2._____

3._____

Name:_____ Age:____

Address:_____

_____

_____

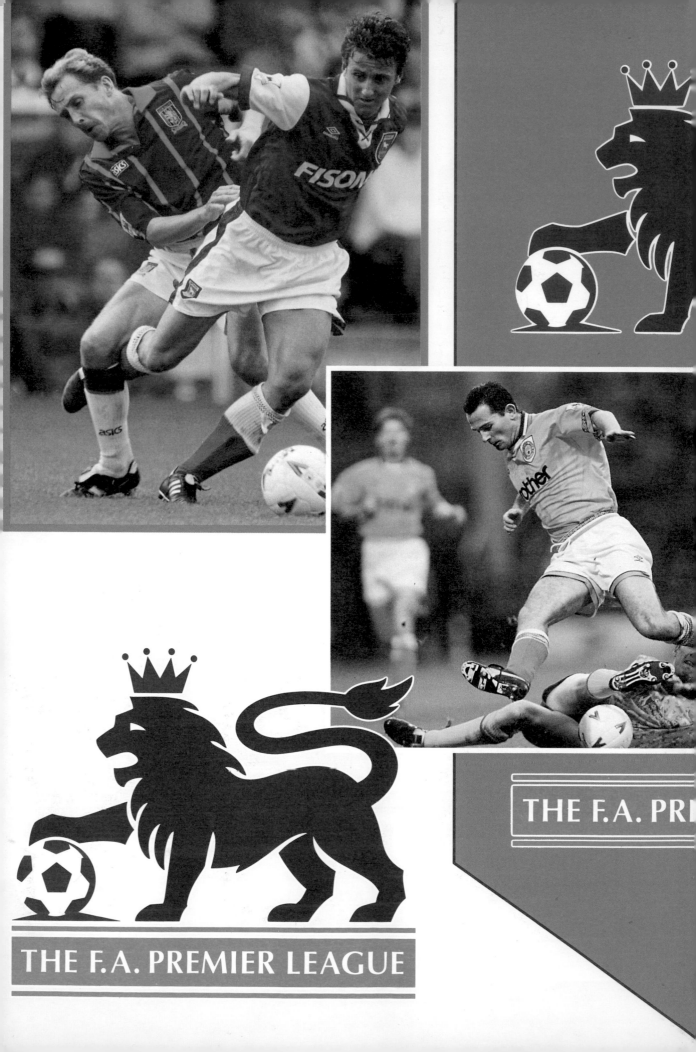

THE F.A. PREMIER LEAGUE

THE F.A. PR